I

♡ u

Alfie

Written by Stewart Allan

Edited by Nicola Baxter
Design by Zoe Bradley
Cover illustrations by Lauren Farnsworth

First published in Great Britain in 2015 by Buster Books, an imprint of Michael O'Mara Books Limited, 9 Lion Yard, Tremadoc Road, London SW4 7NQ

Artwork adapted from www.shutterstock.com

Andrews McMeel Publishing, LLC
an Andrews McMeel Universal company
1130 Walnut Street, Kansas City, Missouri 64106

www.andrewsmcmeel.com

15 16 17 18 19 RRD 10 9 8 7 6 5 4 3 2

ISBN: 978-1-4494-7184-2

Library of Congress Control Number: 2015939466

ATTENTION: SCHOOLS AND BUSINESSES
Andrews McMeel books are available at quantity discounts with bulk purchase for educational, business, or sales promotional use. For information, please e-mail the Andrews McMeel Publishing Special Sales Department: specialsales@amuniversal.com.

PLEASE NOTE: This book is not affiliated with or endorsed by Alfie Deyes or any of his publishers or licensees.

I ♥ Alfie

Andrews McMeel
Publishing®

Kansas City · Sydney · London

Contents

About this book

Alfie Deyes has become one of the most famous faces on the Internet over the last few years and he has won a legion of followers just by being himself. Millions of viewers around the world just can't get enough of his cheeky charm and "pointless" challenges.

If you can't help scribbling "I Heart Alfie" on everything you own, you probably know loads about him and his vlogger pals already. Maybe you've even thought about vlogging yourself.

This book is packed with quizzes and puzzles that will test your knowledge about Alfie and his chums, crazy challenges for you to try with your friends, and lots of handy tips about how to start your own vlog. Who knows, you too could be an online sensation one day!

Good luck. And remember: be as pointless as possible!

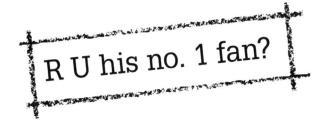

R U his no. 1 fan?

YOU MIGHT THINK YOU KNOW EVERYTHING ABOUT ALFIE AND HIS POINTLESSBLOG CHANNELS, BUT ARE YOU REALLY 100% SURE YOU HAVE ALL THE FACTS? TAKE THIS MULTIPLE-CHOICE QUIZ AND FIND OUT IF YOU'RE READY TO CALL YOURSELF ALFIE'S NO. 1 FAN OR IF YOU STILL HAVE SOME STUDYING TO DO. CHECK YOUR ANSWERS ON **PAGE 91**, THEN TURN TO **PAGE 9** FOR YOUR FAN-FACT EVALUATION.

1. Which female singer did Alfie collaborate with on a couple of videos in October 2013?

   a. Jessie J

   b. Ariana Grande

   c. Rita Ora

2. What age was Alfie when he posted his first PointlessBlog video on YouTube?

   a. 15

   b. 16

   c. 17

3. Alfie talked about the Charlieissocoollike video
channel in his first PointlessBlog video. Do you
know the real name of the vlogger who posts as
Charlieissocoollike?

a. Charlie Brown

b. Charlie McDougal

c. Charlie McDonnell

4. In Alfie's "My 21st Birthday!" video, one of Zoe's
guinea pigs takes a shower in the kitchen sink. Can
you name which one?

a. Pippin

b. Pingu

c. Percy

5. Which one of these helpful hints appears in Alfie's
"7 Ways To Improve YOUR Life!" video?

a. Always look on the bright side of life.

b. Build your own dreams instead of somebody else's.

c. Don't forget your toothbrush.

6. When Alfie's *The Pointless Book* signing tour was
postponed in September 2014 because so many fans
were queuing up to meet him, which London venue
played host to the first rescheduled date?

a. Waterstones, Piccadilly Circus

b. The O_2

c. ExCeL London

7. What is the name of the online chat show Alfie hosts alongside Jim Chapman, Marcus Butler, and Caspar Lee?

   a. Loose Boys

   b. The Crew

   c. You Talk

8. When Alfie and Marcus took the Guinness World Records OMG! Challenge to eat as many bananas as possible in one minute, what was their combined total?

   a. 3

   b. 6

   c. 8

9. What type of dog does Alfie own?

   a. A Pug

   b. A Jack Russell

   c. An Alsation

10. Which of these epic fails does Alfie talk about in his "What NOT To Do At A Festival Ad"?

   a. At Glastonbury he forgot where his tent was and spent the whole night looking for it.

   b. Someone stole his hat when he dropped it in an Enter Shikari mosh pit.

   c. He dropped his phone into a portable toilet and had to use a sock on his hand to fish it out.

11. On whose radio show did Alfie play "Call or Delete" in November 2014?

    a. Chris Evans

    b. Dermot O'Leary

    c. Nick Grimshaw

12. What name does Alfie's pal Joe Sugg use when he's vlogging?

    a. ThatcherJoe

    b. JoeMighty

    c. Suggles

SUPER-FAN SCORECARD

Score 0–4: You're a chump (not a chum)
Do you even know who Alfie is? Luckily, there's an easy solution: Watch more Alfie!

Score 5–9: You're a no. 1 prospect
Keep up the good work. You've covered the basics, but step up your fan-time if you want to win the crown.

Score 10–12: You're a no. 1 fan
Go to the top of the class! Reward yourself by watching more Alfie videos and reading *The Pointless Book*.

Favorite things

ALFIE FILLS HIS VIDEOS WITH HIS LIKES AND DISLIKES. TAKE THE QUIZ BELOW AND FIND OUT HOW MUCH YOU KNOW ABOUT ALFIE'S FAVORITE THINGS. CHECK HOW YOU DID BY LOOKING AT THE ANSWERS ON **PAGE 91**.

1. What is Alfie's favorite thing to do when he's bored?
   a. Reading celebrity gossip magazines
   b. Going to the fridge
   c. Taking Nala for a walk

2. Which three foods does Alfie like to eat most?
   a. Toast, beans, and cheese
   b. Pizza, salad, and cheesecake
   c. Pasta, Terry's Chocolate Orange, and chicken

3. What was Alfie's favorite activity on his trip to Dubai?
   a. Spending the day visiting the Royal Palaces
   b. Swimming in a giant tank with sharks
   c. Driving around the city in a stretch limo

4. Which three films does Alfie say are his favorites?
   a. *Dirty Dancing, Grease,* and *Mamma Mia*
   b. *Scary Movie 3, The Truman Show,* and *The Lion King*
   c. *Scream, The Croods,* and *Frozen*

5. Which band does Alfie say he genuinely likes, even though he's a boy?

a. 5 Seconds of Summer

b. Union J

c. One Direction

6. What is Alfie's favorite thing about the summer?

a. Not having to wake up early

b. Having more free time to make his vlogs

c. Being able to stay up late

7. What are Alfie's three favorite personality traits in other people?

a. Being energetic, loud, and excitable

b. Being intelligent, talkative, and thoughtful

c. Being funny, kind, and caring

8. What are the three things Alfie would miss the most if he didn't have them?

a. Nala, his pug; his flat; and Zoe

b. His phone, his family, and his friends

c. His microwave, his hat collection, and his two front teeth

9. What is Alfie genuinely looking forward to about getting older?

a. Having kids and being a dad

b. Not having to worry about what his hair looks like

c. Being able to retire from vlogging

Challenge Alfie!

ALFIE AND HIS VLOGGER PALS HAVE ATTEMPTED
SOME CRAZY STUNTS AND CHALLENGES IN THEIR
YOUTUBE VIDEOS. SET YOUR OWN COMPLETELY
UNPREDICTABLE CHALLENGES FOR ALFIE!
JUST ROLL THE DICE FOR EACH STAGE.

1. Roll the dice to choose the challenge object:

⚀ Egg

⚁ Marshmallow

⚂ Slices of bread

⚃ Pages from a newspaper or blank paper

⚄ M&Ms

⚅ Piece of fruit

2. Roll the dice to show what Alfie has to do:

⚀ Fill a sock

⚁ Balance them on top of each other

⚂ Fill a pillow case

⚁ Hold in one hand and walk around the room

⚃ Fill his pockets

⚄ Throw into a box

3. How long the challenge should last:

⚀ As long as it takes

⚁ 10 seconds

⚂ 30 seconds

⚁ 1 minute

⚃ 3 minutes

⚄ 5 minutes

Use the dice to randomly choose three challenges for Alfie and write them here:

1..

....

2..

....

3..

....

ALFIE LOVES HIS FOLLOWERS TO LOOK GOOD AND HIS MERCHANDISE IS AMAZING. HAVE A GO AT DESIGNING YOUR OWN ALFIE-INSPIRED T-SHIRTS AND BEANIES FOR HIS ONLINE SHOP. USE THE TEMPLATES BELOW TO HELP.

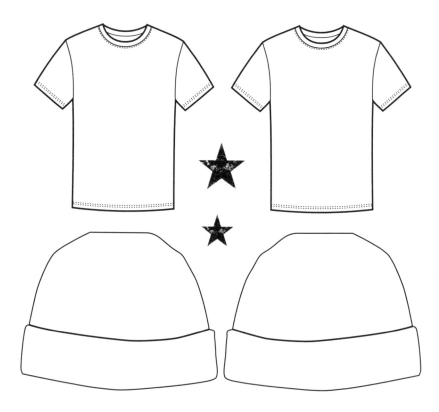

Sweet tweets

ALFIE LIKES TO STAY IN TOUCH WITH HIS MILLIONS OF FOLLOWERS VIA TWITTER. HERE ARE A FEW OF HIS FUNNIEST, SWEETEST, AND MOST INSPIRATIONAL MESSAGES TO YOU, HIS BIGGEST FANS.

You're all so lovely. I wish there was a way that we could meet up, chat & eat food together without it being too busy x

It's amazing to think that you've watched my relationship with @ZozeeBo grow from the first day we met, to now living together with Nala

People who sleep before midnight.. HOW YOU DO IT?!

Remind yourself that you don't have to do what everyone else is doing

No matter how great you are, not everybody will like you. That's life.

I always forget that the word chump means 'a foolish or easily deceived person'. Whenever I call you a chump, I mean it in a loving way ha x

Meet the vloggers

ALFIE ISN'T THE ONLY VLOGGER OUT THERE. IN FACT, ALFIE COUNTS SOME OF THE MOST FAMOUS BLOGGERS AND YOUTUBERS AMONGST HIS CLOSEST FRIENDS. READ ABOUT THEM ON **PAGE 18**. SEE IF YOU CAN WORK OUT WHICH ONE OF ALFIE'S VLOGGER CHUMS SAID WHAT BELOW. CHECK YOUR ANSWERS ON **PAGE 91**.

1. "Going through the stages of an early relationship is actually very daunting for me, now imagine if I was doing that in front of hundreds and thousands, if not millions of people."

Who said it?..

2. "I love that every video can be different. I don't have anyone telling me what to do, and I can travel and do it from anywhere."

Who said it?..

3. "It's the best job in the world by far. And I can say that because I've had some awful jobs."

Who said it?..

4. "People can see I'm just a normal person. I like the same things as them, I have some of the same issues they have, and I guess people feel like they are part of my life."

Who said it?...

5. "I like filming a well-planned sketch. If I have thought about all the shots and there are different characters and costumes, that is a lot of fun because I'm putting in loads of effort."

Who said it?...

6. "I wanted a creative outlet. I just thought it was fun. I had no idea it could be a career or a business."

Who said it?...

7. "Offline is important, but online is the future."

Who said it?...

8. "John Cleese asked lots of good questions about what we do on YouTube. He said he'd tried to do YouTube himself, but it's not really his demographic."

Who said it?...

9. "My appeal is that I'm just a friendly down-to-earth girl, with a standard upbringing, who likes cups of tea and Lush baths."

Who said it?...

MEET THE VLOGGERS

Zoe Sugg, aka Zoella, is probably the most famous vlogger of them all ... and she just happens to be Alfie's girlfriend. Zoe specializes in making videos about fashion and makeup but can turn her hand to just about anything.

Marcus Butler and Alfie became pals after watching each other's YouTube videos. They love challenging each other to play silly games or perform ridiculous stunts.

Tanya Burr is a trained makeup artist whose tutorials on how to apply makeup and advice about which are the best and most value-for-money brands have brought her fame as well as her own range of lip glosses and nail polishes.

Caspar Lee grew up in South Africa before moving to the UK. He is best known for his pranks and creating weird comedy characters. He shares a flat with Zoe's vlogger brother, Joe (aka ThatcherJoe).

Jim Chapman spent a long time trying to find the perfect job before posting his first YouTube video. He started out as the male Zoella, offering fashion and style tips to men, before branching out into more advice-based videos.

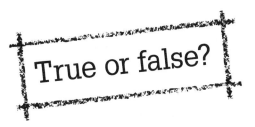 

ALFIE HAS HAD SOME SERIOUSLY CRAZY STORIES TO TELL YOU IN HIS VIDEOS. DO YOU KNOW WHICH OF THE TALL TALES LISTED BELOW ARE TRUE AND WHICH ARE FALSE? HERE'S A CLUE: THERE'S ONLY ONE BIG, FAT FIB. SEE IF YOU SPOTTED IT ON **PAGE 92**.

1. Once Alfie asked a fan he met to hold his camera. When he turned back to her, she was sucking the microphone on the top of it.

☐ True ☐ False

2. At a festival, the toilets were so disgusting that Alfie paid £15 to use the VIP ones. The toilet looked like a royal throne, so he had his picture taken sitting on it.

☐ True ☐ False

3. When Alfie was little he was stung on the arm by a bee while in the bath. The bee died and fell into the bath.

☐ True ☐ False

4. At his first concert, Alfie got dragged into the mosh pit and, a bit over-excited, elbowed a big guy in the chest, only to be punched in the face in return.

☐ True ☐ False

Love it or hate it?

ALFIE HAS BEEN VERY CLEAR ON HIS POINTLESSBLOG ABOUT HIS LIKES AND DISLIKES. HE'S EVEN MADE SOME VIDEOS SPECIFICALLY ABOUT THE THINGS HE LOVES AND THE THINGS HE HATES. CAN YOU TELL WHETHER THESE STATEMENTS ARE TRUE OR FALSE? FIND THE ANSWERS ON **PAGE 92**.

1. One of Alfie's biggest dislikes is getting out of bed in the morning.

☐ True   ☐ False

2. Alfie doesn't really believe in superstitions, but he doesn't take chances with any of them just in case.

☐ True   ☐ False

3. Alfie really loves to watch *I'm a Celebrity... Get Me Out of Here!*

☐ True   ☐ False

4. Alfie's favorite animals are monkeys.

☐ True   ☐ False

5. Alfie likes using a PC rather than an Apple Mac.

☐ True ☐ False

6. Alfie's favorite places in the world are Brighton, Greece, and Dubai.

☐ True ☐ False

7. Alfie dislikes people who walk really slowly in front of him.

☐ True ☐ False

8. Alfie really likes girls who smile a lot.

☐ True ☐ False

9. Alfie's favorite thing about school was wearing a school uniform.

☐ True ☐ False

10. One of Alfie's favorite foods is Terry's Chocolate Oranges.

☐ True ☐ False

11. Alfie really likes public displays of affection.

☐ True ☐ False

Getting started

ALFIE WAS ONLY 15 YEARS OLD WHEN HE STARTED HIS POINTLESSBLOG WAY BACK IN 2009. ONE OF THE FIRST BLOGGERS TO HAVE HIS OWN CHANNEL ON YOUTUBE, HE HAS MANAGED TO BUILD A MASSIVE FAN BASE VERY QUICKLY. WOULD YOU LIKE TO BECOME A HUGE INTERNET STAR LIKE ALFIE? HERE ARE SOME TOP TIPS ABOUT HOW TO GET STARTED WITH YOUR OWN BLOG OR VLOG AND THE IMPORTANCE OF STAYING SAFE ONLINE.

1. **Decide if you want to start a blog or a vlog.**
   If you are shy about appearing on camera or really enjoy writing, perhaps the best idea is to begin with a written blog. Blogging is much more straightforward and requires less equipment and technological know-how. Writing a blog will increase your knowledge about your chosen subject, help you understand what makes it interesting for your readers, and may give you the extra confidence needed to make the jump to vlogging.

   Vlogging requires a little more effort and you will need access to a few bits of important equipment before you begin: You will need a camera to record your videos — this can be anything from the most expensive digital cameras to the video setting on your phone. Some of the most famous YouTube video stars, including 5 Seconds of Summer, started out by recording their videos with iPhones.

You will also need some video-editing software. Your videos will be much better and look more professional if you edit them before you post them online. Remember, not even Alfie gets everything right all the time. Most laptops and computers have video-editing software pre-installed, but there are more sophisticated versions available. Watch a few online tutorials about the software you are using so you know exactly what your system can do.

You will need to have somewhere to post your videos. YouTube is probably the most popular video platform, but there are others and the biggest one may not be the most appropriate one for your vlog.

2. **Decide what you want your blog/vlog to be about.** It's always best to write or talk about something you have been excited about for a long time. If you are really passionate about a certain subject, know a lot about it, and want to share it with others, your enthusiasm will be obvious in your posts. The best subjects offer lots of different areas you can talk about. A narrow subject means there might be less to talk about and fewer people who might be interested.

3. **Look at other blogs/vlogs.**
You want your blog/vlog to reflect who you are and to be as original as possible. Take a look at the competition. If you think your posts might be too similar to someone else's, you'd be better going back to the drawing board. Having something fresh and exciting to say, even if it's a popular subject like fashion or food, is essential when starting out.

4. **Be prepared and organized.**
When you are just starting out, it's very important to do your research. Make sure you are confident and knowledgeable about your subject and have a definite plan about what you are going to say. Make lots of notes. It's not a problem if you think you need to follow a script — not everyone is good at making things up as they go along. Keep practicing. Do plenty of test posts or videos before you put anything online. Show them to your friends or family if you want an outside opinion. Other people can often see things you miss, and it's always good to get a different viewpoint.

5. **Have fun!**
There is no point writing a blog or filming your own videos if you're not having fun while you do it. If you are worried or stressed, your readers and viewers will pick up on it and may not come back. If you're relaxed and having a good time, your audience will enjoy themselves too.

SAFETY ONLINE

Sometimes the Internet can be a dangerous place, and it's easy to forget there might be millions of people reading your posts or watching your videos. Here are a few very simple and easy things to do to make sure you stay safe when you are online.

Never give out personal information, such as your mobile phone number, home phone number, or your home address, in your blogs or vlogs.

Don't share your passwords or other forms of security protection with anyone, including your best friend, and especially with people online.

Always check every social media site's privacy settings, and make sure you activate or deactivate the functions you want to apply to your posts.

Think twice about anything you post online. Some things should be private, so always be certain you want other people to see your photographs or the things you've written. Also, make sure you have the permission to post group photos from everyone in the picture.

Do not arrange to meet anyone in person who you first "meet" online. People may not be who you think they are or who they say they are.

Don't post rude or offensive things online. A good rule is: If you wouldn't say something to someone in person, don't post it online.

Don't download or install any software onto your computer or phone unless you have checked it is safe.

If anything you read or see online makes you uncomfortable or you think it may be dangerous, speak to a parent, guardian, or teacher about it right away.

Never reply to any rude texts, messages, or emails. If you don't want people to comment on your blog or vlog, you should make sure this function is disabled before you start posting. If you do allow comments, don't respond to anything negative, threatening, or offensive. Delete persistent negative comments and block people if they bother you or post things you think are inappropriate.

If you're unsure about anything about the Internet or posting online, speak to your parents, guardians, teachers, or friends about it first.

Keep your private life private. Alfie and Zoe share loads of things with their loyal fans — but not everything. There are plenty of things that they decide not to blog or vlog about while they are happening, as they showed with their decisions on the Zalfie question. Be professional about your blogging and be sure you want to share what you are posting. Remember, it may be seen by the shopkeeper down the road, your mom, or a future employer.

Pointless!

INSPIRED BY ALFIE'S VERY OWN CHANNEL AND BOOK, HERE IS A LIST OF TOTALLY POINTLESS THINGS YOU COULD DO THE NEXT TIME YOU'RE BORED.

1. Move a whole bag of M&Ms from one bowl to another using chopsticks. You can eat them when you're done!

2. Wear one item of clothing inside out for an entire day.

3. Take a random book. Turn to page 10. Look at the 5th line on the page. Find the 3rd word in that line. Use this word in your next text, tweet, or conversation.

4. Spend a whole day without saying the word *No*.

5. Challenge a friend to a race to write the whole alphabet in mirror-writing. You must be able to read every letter correctly and in the right order in a mirror.

6. Who can eat the most baked beans in a minute using a toothpick, you or your friend?

7. Draw a picture of the best thing that happened to you today.

What's your dream theme?

Start
You need to decide a subject for your blog or vlog. Which are you?

Artistic. You like to be creative and make things.

There's a party at your place tonight. What's your priority?

Getting into the kitchen and baking loads of snacks for your ravenous friends.

Dashing out to a just-open boutique for a fab show-stealing outfit.

Curious. You like adventure and finding new things.

You've got a free weekend. What would you rather do?

Take a trip to somewhere you heard is the place to be seen.

Set off on a movie marathon, seeing all the films you've missed lately.

You're cooking up a storm. What are you making?

Tasty treats that are good for you, too. You can't dance all night on fast-food fuel.

You should vlog about FOOD
Not only can you show how to cook delicious dishes, you're a guru of healthy goodness, too. You've got a lot to say!

A feast of fusion flavors worthy of a celebrity chef.

You should vlog about FASHION
You're interested in the latest, greatest trends in clothes, makeup, food, places, and people. Who wouldn't want to hear your tips and tricks?

Yes, it's a trendy spot, but what really interests you there?

It's crawling with celebrities after the latest looks. You fit right in!

The place has a fascinating history and the locals are great.

You should vlog about TRAVEL
You've got an adventurous spirit and an eye for detail. With so many stories to tell, what's stopping you?

How to get to the cinemas and what the popcorn is like.

You want to get online right away. What do you tell your friends?

Which movies to see and why they're great.

You should vlog about CINEMA
You're a real fan and you've seen everything there is to see. You can help film fans dodge the flops but catch the crackers.

Quirky questions

ALFIE IS ALWAYS KEEN TO KEEP IN TOUCH WITH HIS VIEWERS AND ANSWER THEIR QUESTIONS — EVEN WHEN THEY MIGHT SEEM A LITTLE STRANGE. CAN YOU MATCH THE QUESTIONS BELOW WITH ALFIE'S ANSWERS? TO MAKE IT TRICKIER, A COUPLE OF THE ANSWERS ARE FAKE. CHECK **PAGE 92** TO FIND OUT HOW YOU DID.

Questions from viewers:

1. "What face did you pull when you heard One Direction's 'Little Things'?"

2. "Would you rather have ten-inch eyelashes or an eyebrow that goes all the way around your head?"

3. "What's the strangest thing fans have challenged you to do?"

4. "Aside from being a YouTuber, if you could do any job in the world, what would it be?"

5. "What's the weirdest fan experience you've ever had?"

6. "Why did you wear red socks?"

Alfie's answers:

A. "It would be really sick to be able to ... see into the future."

B. "Mine pretty much do that anyway."

C. "She sat next to me on the train and the whole time she was like, 'Why are you wearing girl's shoes? You've got fluff on your jeans. Do you want me to get that off?'"

D. "I used to want to be, like I don't even know why, a dentist."

E. "I think I did the fangirl dance. I think I full-on did the dance! Flailed my arms, was screaming ... I even cried."

F. "A girl wrote in mashed potato on a plate and was scared someone would eat it before I managed to read it."

G. "I don't know, just pointless things, like Zoe waxing my legs."

H. "Someone actually tried to shake my hand while I was in an airport bathroom ... and it wasn't another boy."

I. "I didn't think anyone was going to see."

Write your answers here:

1. .... **3.** .... **5.** ....

2. .... **4.** .... **6.** ....

How romantic ...

ALFIE AND ZOE HAVE BEEN TOGETHER FOR A WHILE NOW AND THEIR FOLLOWERS HAVE BEEN WITH THEM EVERY STEP OF THE WAY. TAKE A LOOK AT THE FOLLOWING QUOTES AND STATEMENTS ABOUT ZALFIE'S RELATIONSHIP AND RATE THEM BY COLORING IN THE BLANK HEART SHAPES.

How romantic?

 Cold-Hearted But Cute

 Weird But Wonderful

 Super Sweet

 Swoon

 Perfect Love

In February 2013, Alfie said the following when he was making the "My Valentines Date" video with Zoe: "We're not in a relationship. We're not together. We wouldn't be cute together. We're not going to get married ... None of that guys, we're literally two friends making a video together for you."

When Zoe asked Alfie, "Do you think love exists?" Alfie said: "I think relationship-wise, with a girl, obviously if you've been with somebody for like, I dunno, ten years and you have kids and you're married, then obviously you love them."

In the same video, Zoe asked Alfie, "Does age matter when you're in love?" He replied, "I dunno, I would say usually it does, but then the other day I was walking down the street and I saw this woman and I was like, 'I think I love her. I think I genuinely love her.' I realized she was 96! Is that bad?"

During the "Cooking Zoe Dinner FAIL!" video, Alfie said to Zoe: "I'm going to make my own pasta, just for myself, bye ... I'm going to eat it all!"

During his "Sleeping With My Crush..." video, Alfie pretends to have a secret date with a life-size Emma Watson pillow and says: "We can't tell Zoe this is going on."

During his "Im The Best Boyfriend EVER!" video, Alfie made a late-night trip to Zoe's flat after he'd been out with a pal. He said, "I bought Zoe a Nando's 'cos she's tucked up in bed."

After Alfie had given Zoe her food, he told her he wasn't staying and was heading back to his flat to play video games with his pal.

In early December 2014, Alfie decided to show his support to Zoe by taking some time away from vlogging. He said, "We've both been so busy recently working on different things so a little break will do us good as we haven't spent proper time together x."

In Alfie's "Tickle Fight With Zoella" video, Zoe gives Alfie a back massage with a meat pounder.

In the same video, Zoe says she really wants to see Alfie take part in the TV show *Release the Hounds*. Isn't that the show where people have to outrun a group of vicious, giant dogs as they chase them and they have to run for their lives?

In the video "Kissing Another YouTuber..." when asked, "Would you rather stop YouTubing or never see Zoe again?" Alfie shows a shot of himself packing Zoe's case!

On October 17, 2014, the day they moved in together, Alfie said moving in with Zoe was their "exciting thing" to do in private together.

In the same video, Alfie's response to the thought of announcing that Zalfie were getting married was, "No! Just NO! No, No, No!"

Up for a challenge

ALFIE AND HIS YOUTUBER PALS ARE ALWAYS UP FOR A CHALLENGE. SOME ARE FUNNY, OTHERS ARE JUST RIDICULOUS. HERE'S A LIST OF CRAZY CHALLENGES FOR YOU TO TAKE EITHER ON YOUR OWN OR WITH SOME OF YOUR BEST FRIENDS. GOOD LUCK!

Take the Blindfold Drawing Challenge
Draw a picture while you're wearing a blindfold (or with your eyes shut tight). If you do this challenge with friends, make sure you all pick the same subject—self portraits, draw each other, things in the room, or the same famous person. You can also set a time limit to make it even funnier.

Take the Worst Selfie Challenge
Everyone has to take a selfie while pulling a funny face. You then have to decide which one is the worst.

Take the Chubby Bunny Challenge

For this challenge, you'll need some big bags of marshmallows. Each person must take it in turn to put a marshmallow in his mouth and then say the words, "chubby bunny." Don't eat the marshmallow! After everyone has taken a turn, you go around the group again and each person has to put another marshmallow in his mouth and say, "chubby bunny." Remember, no eating! Keep going and each person who can't fit another marshmallow in his mouth or can't say "chubby bunny" is eliminated until you have a clear (chubby bunny–looking) winner.

There are loads of silly, funny, outrageous challenges you can take—as Alfie has shown! Write down some of your own ideas here.

....

....

....

....

....

....

....

....

★★★★★★★★★★★

Love by numbers

COULD YOU AND ALFIE BE SOUL MATES? JUST FOR FUN,
SEE WHAT THE SUMS SAY.

Write your name and his with the word *LOVES* in the middle. Then write down how many times the letters *L*, *O*, *V*, *E*, and *S* appear in both your names in a line—but don't include the letters from *LOVES*. Add together pairs of numbers—the first and the second, the second and the third, and so on—to work out a final "percentage." This tells you how likely you are to be fast friends with Alfie.

Here's an example:

AMY MORRIS LOVES ALFIE DEYES

There are one *L*, one *O*, zero *V*s, three *E*s, and two *S*s. Write this as: 1 1 0 3 2. Add together each pair of numbers until you have only two left. If a sum has a two-digit number (like 12), just write it as two numbers: 1 2.

1 1 0 3 2

2 1 3 5

3 4 8

7 1 2

8 3

83%

ALFIE STARTED VLOGGING WHEN HE WAS 15 YEARS OLD,
BUT IT LOOKS LIKE HE HAS ALWAYS BEEN DESTINED
TO BE A STAR. ANSWER THE QUESTIONS BELOW ABOUT
ALFIE'S CHILDHOOD YEARS AND FIND OUT HOW MUCH
YOU KNOW ABOUT HIM BEFORE HE WAS FAMOUS.
CHECK YOUR ANSWERS ON **PAGE 92**.

1. Which video game did Alfie say took up most of his childhood?

  a. Super Mario Kart

  b. The Legend of Zelda

  c. Pokémon

2. What did Alfie admit to stealing from his local Ikea store?

  a. Mini pencils

  b. Candles

  c. Shopping trolleys

3. What was the job Alfie told his mom he wanted to do when he grew up?

  a. Working as a zoo keeper looking after monkeys

  b. Picking up dog poo in parks

  c. A lifeguard at his local swimming pool

4. What kind of animal was Alfie's childhood pet Smidge?

a. Angora rabbit

b. Nelson's milksnake

c. Tarantula spider

5. Alfie has admitted his family owns a video of him wearing a dress while singing and dancing along to songs by which pop group?

a. S Club 7

b. Spice Girls

c. Girls Aloud

6. What kind of family holiday did Alfie enjoy most when he was younger?

a. Going camping

b. Boat trips

c. Staying at home

7. What did Alfie say he believed in when he was a child?

a. Unicorns

b. Fairies

c. Dragons

8. Where did Alfie's mom and dad *say* they first met?

a. Online on a dating site

b. At the circus where Alfie's mom was a trapeze artist

c. At a restaurant where Alfie's dad was a chef

9. When Alfie was about six, what did he do to his dad while he was asleep?

  a. Shaved a spiral into the hair on the back of his head

  b. Drew cat whiskers on his face with permanent pen

  c. Tied his shoelaces together so he fell over when he stood up

10. When Alfie was about ten, he saw his friend cheat at a competition they were both taking part in. What happened?

  a. Alfie told the judges, his friend was disqualified, and they never talked to each other again.

  b. Alfie said nothing and his friend won the competition. Alfie came second.

  c. Alfie's mom saw his friend cheating and started shouting at him during the competition.

11. Alfie says he didn't have a "proper" one of these until he was 14 or 15. What was it?

  a. Girlfriend

  b. Camera

  c. Motorbike

12. What does Alfie say has always stopped him getting to sleep?

  a. Birds singing outside the window

  b. Wearing socks in bed

  c. Eating pizza at midnight

What vlog?

SOMETIMES ALFIE'S VLOGS CAN BE A BIT
CONFUSING. READ THE QUOTES BELOW AND TRY TO
WORK OUT WHO OR WHAT ALFIE IS TALKING ABOUT.
EXTRA POINTS IF YOU CAN ACTUALLY NAME THE
VLOG THEY ARE FROM. FIND THE ANSWERS
ON **PAGE 93**.

1. "This morning .... decided to cry because
she needed the toilet, which is fair enough, but she
decided to cry at 6:55. So I had to get out of bed at
6:55 after going to bed at half past 3."

Who is Alfie talking about? ....

Which vlog? ....

2. "Feels weird. It's not very big but it's getting there,
okay. It's getting there and that's the important thing."

What is Alfie talking about? ....

Which vlog? ....

3. "Like, literally felt like my teeth were going to fall out eating some of them."

What is Alfie talking about? ....

Which vlog? ....

4. "If you need to cut it, I'm using one hand so it's a lot harder, cut it with scissors rather than a knife. It's sooooooo much easier."

What is Alfie talking about? ....

Which vlog? ....

5. "I never actually tried it and people were like, 'Wow, you've never tried it? Oh, wow, that's like awesome.' And I'm like, 'You lot were trying it when you were younger thinking it was cool and now I'm like the one who's getting the good reputation for not ever trying it.'"

What is Alfie talking about? ....

Which vlog? ....

6. "Very, very, very nice guy. I've known him since 300 subscribers, from watching his videos. He puts a lot of time and work in. He works really, really hard and he is very, very successful."

What is Alfie talking about? ....

Which vlog? ....

TRY THIS FUN GAME AND LET FATE DECIDE WHAT YOU
DO WITH ALFIE ON A TOTALLY UNPREDICTABLE FEW
HOURS OUT TOGETHER. YOU'LL NEED DICE TO PLAY
ALONG. SIMPLY THROW THE DICE AND WHATEVER
NUMBER COMES UP DECIDES THE NEXT STAGE OF YOUR
ADVENTURE. GO ON, ROLL WITH IT!

A. How do you get in touch with Alfie to arrange your date?
1. Facebook **2.** Text **3.** Twitter **4.** Instagram **5.** Post a
YouTube video **6.** Postcard

B. What time are you meeting Alfie?
1. 10 am **2.** Midday **3.** 2 pm **4.** 5 pm **5.** 8 pm **6.** Midnight

C. What are you going to wear?
1. Prom dress **2.** School uniform **3.** T-shirt and jeans
4. Fancy dress **5.** Onesie **6.** Wetsuit

D. Where have you decided to go together?
1. London **2.** Brighton **3.** Paris **4.** Your house **5.** Alfie's
place **6.** Your school

E. What are you going to do there?
1. Make challenge videos **2.** Go to a fancy restaurant
3. Get Nando's takeaway **4.** Watch a movie **5.** Walk on
the beach **6.** Go to an adventure water park

F. What present has Alfie brought you?
1. Some of his merchandise **2.** A signed *The Pointless Book*
3. A pug puppy **4.** Sweets and candies **5.** A camera and microphone **6.** His favorite T-shirt

G. Alfie wants to make a quick stop-off before you head out. Who does he take you to meet?
1. His mom **2.** Nala **3.** Zoe **4.** Marcus Butler **5.** Jamie Oliver **6.** His dentist

H. You have a great time. What does Alfie whisper as you say goodbye?
1. "I'm so glad I met you. You're special." **2.** "See ya! Wouldn't wanna be ya!" **3.** "Do you want to do this again sometime?" **4.** "I think I love you." **5.** "Can I borrow a pound for my bus fare?" **6.** "Does your mom really have to come next time?"

If your dice-rolling doesn't give you the results you'd like, note down your dream meeting with Alfie here:

I'm going to meet Alfie ....

Together, we will ....

As a present, he will give me ....

He'll even take me to meet ....

He'll tell me ....

....

Up close and personal

?

TAKE THESE QUICK-FIRE QUIZZES AND SEE HOW MUCH YOU KNOW ABOUT ALFIE, ZALFIE, AND ALFIE'S FRIENDS AND FAMILY. WRITE YOUR ANSWERS AS QUICKLY AS POSSIBLE AND TIME YOURSELF IF YOU CAN. YOU'LL FIND THE ANSWERS ON **PAGE 93**. CAN YOU DO BETTER THAN YOUR FRIENDS?

All about Alfie

1. Where does Alfie live? ....

2. What is the name of his pet pug? ....

3. Name Alfie's bestselling book. ....

4. What is Alfie's star sign? ....

5. What year did Alfie start his YouTube channel? ....

6. How many party-poppers did Alfie pop in 30 seconds to win a Guinness World Record? ....

7. In his "Googling Myself" video, what was the first search result after he typed "Is Alfie Deyes ..."?

....

8. In which month is Alfie's birthday? ....

TOTAL SCORE .... TIME TAKEN ....

● ● ● ● ● ● ● ● ● ● ● ● ● ● ● ● ● ●

All about Zalfie

1. What are Zoe's pet guinea pigs called? ....
....

2. Name Zoe's first novel. ....

3. Name the blog entry in which Zoe revealed she was
dating Alfie. ....

4. During which month in 2013 did Alfie and Zoe
officially announce they were dating? ....

5. Is Zoe's brother older or younger than her? ....

6. What is the tagline of Zoe's online blog? ....
....

7. What is Zoe's favorite book? ....

8. Where does "Zoe" say she first met Alfie in Alfie's "The
Girlfriend Tag!" video? ....

TOTAL SCORE .... TIME TAKEN ....

All about Alfie's family and friends

1. What is Alfie's sister's name? ....

2. Name one of the other vloggers who regularly joins Alfie as part of "The Crew." ....

3. What do Alfie and his vlogger pals call the Advent period running up to Christmas? ....

4. At which university did Alfie's sister study?

....

5. Which male vlogger has a female alter ego called Margaret? ....

6. What is the name of Louise Pentland's vlogger channel?

....

7. Which high-street retailer helped Tanya Burr launch her own cosmetics range?

....

8. What is the name of the tour Alfie and his vlogger pals took part in during October 2014? ....

TOTAL SCORE .... TIME TAKEN ....

Your day with Alfie

IMAGINE ALFIE IS HEADED TO NEW YORK FOR A SPECIAL VLOGGER EVENT AND WANTS TO SHARE THE EXPERIENCE WITH HIS NUMBER-ONE FAN. TO WIN THIS FAB PRIZE, ALL YOU HAVE TO DO IS POST A VIDEO DESCRIBING THE ULTIMATE FUN WEEKEND YOU CAN'T WAIT TO TRY! FILL IN THE GAPS IN THE STORY BELOW, USING THE WORDS IN BRACKETS OR ADDING YOUR OWN, TO CREATE YOUR OWN BLOG/VLOG OF WHAT HAPPENED NEXT.

You're determined to win that fantastic trip and manage to post your video on the day before the competition closes. Your vlog starts with you telling Alfie your ideal weekend with him would take place in ...., (Paris/ London/ Brighton) and he would need to bring his .... (swimming trunks/ tuxedo/ camera). You'd be spending the evening .... (at the theater/ at a photographer's studio/ at a party with your friends).

The vlog ends with you and Alfie .... (chilling out in front of the TV/ on the red carpet at a premiere/ posting the video of your weekend on Alfie's YouTube channel).

Wow! Alfie loves your story more than any of the others and gets in touch to tell you he's chosen you as his VIP guest on his New York trip. Alfie said the thing he liked

the most about your vlog was ....
(your eyes/ the way you made him laugh/ your accent), and he
loved it so much he's decided you can bring three friends
with you on the trip. Choosing just three is hard but you

know that .... , ... , and ....
will love it and add to the fun.

Alfie lets you know that on your first night in New York you
will be attending a very fancy party, which is being held in

his honor to celebrate ....
(his *The Pointless Book* sales/ the fact he has been voted "Best
Vlogger EVER!"/ his engagement to Zoe), and you need to wear
something extra special. You decide you really don't have

anything suitable to wear so you ....

.... (rush out to buy a whole new wardrobe/
borrow a designer dress from a friend/ ask Alfie if he will take
you shopping in New York).

For the next week, your trip to New York with Alfie is all
you can talk about. You spend every night messaging your
three special friends about coordinating your outfits and
decide to wear matching T-shirts on the flight that say

.... (Pug Life/ Your Hair Is
Just Fine/ We're All About Alfie).

On the day of the flight to New York, you meet up with your
friends at the airport. When Alfie joins you in the first-
class departure lounge, your first reaction is to

....

(start shaking/ feel your stomach doing somersaults/ stand staring and speechless). **Alfie is excited to meet everyone and, of course, he's filming everything for a very special PointlessBlog video.**

When you arrive in New York, you are taken to the hotel and shown your rooms, which have an amazing view of

.... (Central Park/ the Empire State Building/ the whole of Manhattan).

Alfie has a couple of important meetings in the afternoon and says he'll join you in a few hours. In the meantime,

....

(Marcus Butler and Jim Chapman/Zoe Sugg and Tanya Burr/ Joe Sugg and Caspar Lee) **will look after you and show you the sights. On a mad dash around the city you visit**

....

(add your must-see New York locations here).

It's almost time to get ready for Alfie's special party and everyone has gone to their rooms to get dressed. Just as you're about to leave, there's a knock at the door. It's Alfie. He's come to give you a very special gift. He hands you

.... (a camera/ a necklace/ Nando's takeaway)

and says .... (What's up, guys?/ I want you to keep this with you forever./ Sorry about my hair!).

The party is in full swing when you arrive. On stage,
.... (your favorite band or singer) **is singing,**

and you spot lots of famous faces in the crowd. Alfie is the perfect host. He never leaves your side and introduces you to everyone as .... (his new best friend/ the most amazing vlogger he's met/ the coolest person in the room).

The next morning you are invited to have a very special breakfast with Alfie in a diner near the hotel. Alfie orders a giant plate of pancakes, and there is a very special message written in chocolate sauce on the top one. It says, ... ("Best trip ever!"/ "Thank you!"/ "I'll never forget you!").

On the flight back, you are sitting with your friends and you tell them that your favorite part of the trip was

....

The next day, Alfie posts his new vlog on his PointlessBlog channel and you're over the moon because he's called it

....

You couldn't have put it better yourself! You only have one word to describe the experience. It was absolutely

....!

Did you know that?

LISTED BELOW ARE SOME AMAZING FACTS ABOUT ALFIE
AND HIS LIFE THAT HE'S SHARED ONLINE. WE'VE ADDED
A FEW MADE-UP STORIES OF OUR OWN, SO PUT A TICK
NEXT TO THE THINGS YOU THINK ARE TRUE AND A CROSS
NEXT TO THE BIG, FAT FIBS. CHECK THE ANSWERS ON
PAGE 93 TO SEE IF YOU CAN TELL FACT FROM FICTION.

☐ **1.** Alfie says if he had to pick between never having
pizza again or never seeing his parents again, he'd
choose to keep eating pizza.

☐ **2.** Alfie used to be able to do the splits but when he
tried to do them for his "25 Facts About Me" video, he
experienced an epic fail.

☐ **3.** Alfie's pug, Nala, was given to him by Jamie Oliver
when *his* pet pug had a litter of puppies and Alfie said
he really wanted one.

☐ **4.** When Alfie and Zoe first started dating, they used
the couple name "Alfoe" for about a week until Zoe
pointed out it sounded too much like a type of flower.

☐ **5.** Alfie can solve a Rubik's cube in less than a minute.

☐ **6.** A fan once sent Alfie a box of jelly beans that included centipede- and vomit-flavored beans.

☐ **7.** Alfie and Caspar Lee grew up together and even went to the same school. They appeared in school shows together and teachers told them they would be a famous comedy double-act one day.

☐ **8.** Alfie claims never to have had a "guy crush."

☐ **9.** Alfie once jumped off a bridge that was 170 feet high with only a piece of elastic tied around his ankles.

☐ **10.** Alfie's sister, Poppy, was named after the character Poppy Pomfrey in the Harry Potter books.

☐ **11.** Alfie says he has never smoked a cigarette or tried any kind of illegal drug, although he did admit he'd had alcohol before he was legally the correct age.

☐ **12.** Alfie took a gap year in 2013, and his intention was to go to university in 2014, even though he hadn't decided what subjects he would study.

☐ **13.** Alfie really can't do a Welsh accent.

☐ **14.** In 2014, Alfie was considering taking part in *Strictly Come Dancing* but after he had a few private lessons, he decided he wasn't a natural and turned down the offer.

☐ **15.** Alfie was born with a very noticeable black patch at the front of his hair. He sometimes worries that it will never go gray.

☐ **16.** Alfie tried to be a vegetarian once, but it lasted less than a week before he got involved in a chicken-nugget challenge!

☐ **17.** Alfie says he only ever dated one girl from his school, but she stopped seeing him when he told her he was a YouTuber. She thought it was something to do with skateboarding.

☐ **18.** Alfie met Marcus Butler through YouTube. They liked each other's videos, messaged each other, and decided to start making videos together.

☐ **19.** Alfie first met Zoe because he met her brother Joe at a gaming convention. They became friends, and it was Joe who suggested Alfie should start dating his sister.

☐ **20.** Alfie once went to a Halloween party dressed as Peter Pan. He said the costume was basically a green dress and tights.

☐ **21.** Alfie had to go to court to keep his PointlessBlog name. He had to prove he had used the name before the *Pointless* TV quiz show was ever on television.

☐ **22.** Alfie's parents had never heard of YouTube when he started vlogging. It was only when girls started chasing him in the street that they realized he was famous.

☐ **23.** Alfie says he is a very neat and organized person. He even describes himself as being ever so slightly OCD about it.

Worst day ever!

ALFIE HAS HAD HIS FAIR SHARE OF HECTIC DAYS AND DISAPPOINTMENTS. SOMETIMES IT HELPS TO WRITE ABOUT THE BAD THINGS THAT HAPPEN TO YOU AS WELL AS THE FUN STUFF. YOU NEVER KNOW, YOU MIGHT BE ABLE TO SEE THOSE THINGS DIFFERENTLY NOW OR EVEN LAUGH ABOUT THEM.

Try filling in the spaces below to help you get started.

Make a list of some of the worst and most embarrassing things that have ever happened to you:

....

....

....

....

Did anything good come out of the bad things that happened?

....

....

Who were you with when you had your "worst day ever"?
How did they help?

....

....

Now write a blog post called "My Worst Day Ever." Could
reading it help other people, as Alfie and Zoe often do?

....

....

....

....

....

....

....

....

....

....

....

....

Best of buds

ALFIE AND ZOE HAVE POSTED VIDEOS IN WHICH THEY ASK EACH OTHER A LIST OF QUESTIONS TO FIND OUT HOW WELL THEY REALLY KNOW EACH OTHER. WHY DON'T YOU AND YOUR BFF DO THE SAME? TAKE TURNS ASKING EACH OTHER THE QUESTIONS IN BOLD BELOW. THERE ARE ALSO SOME BLANK SPACES FOR QUESTIONS OF YOUR OWN. ONCE YOU'VE ASKED ALL THE QUESTIONS, FILL IN THE CORRECT ANSWERS AND SEE HOW YOU RATE AS BEST BUDS.

1. What's my favorite color?

Your friend's answer ....

The correct answer ....

Your answer ....

The correct answer ....

♡♡♡♡♡♡♡♡♡♡♡♡♡♡♡♡♡♡♡♡♡♡

2. Which band or singer played at the first concert I ever went to?

Your friend's answer ....

The correct answer ....

Your answer ....

The correct answer ....

♡♡♡♡♡♡♡♡♡♡♡♡♡♡♡♡♡♡♡♡♡

3. Who is my biggest celebrity crush?

Your friend's answer ....

The correct answer ....

Your answer ....

The correct answer ....

♡♡♡♡♡♡♡♡♡♡♡♡♡♡♡♡♡♡♡♡♡

4. Can you name all my pets?

Your friend's answer ....

The correct answer ....

Your answer ....

The correct answer ....

♡♡♡♡♡♡♡♡♡♡♡♡♡♡♡♡♡♡♡♡♡

5. What would be my ideal job?

Your friend's answer ....

The correct answer ....

Your answer ....

The correct answer ....

♡♡♡♡♡♡♡♡♡♡♡♡♡♡♡♡♡♡♡♡♡♡

6. What would I say is my most annoying habit?

Your friend's answer ....

The correct answer ....

Your answer ....

The correct answer ....

♡♡♡♡♡♡♡♡♡♡♡♡♡♡♡♡♡♡♡♡♡♡

7. What color are the walls in my bedroom?

Your friend's answer ....

The correct answer ....

Your answer ....

The correct answer ....

♡♡♡♡♡♡♡♡♡♡♡♡♡♡♡♡♡♡♡♡♡♡

8. What is my favorite song at the moment?

Your friend's answer ....

The correct answer ....

Your answer ....

The correct answer ....

♡♡♡♡♡♡♡♡♡♡♡♡♡♡♡♡♡♡♡♡♡♡♡♡

9. (Your own question) ....

....

Your friend's answer ....

The correct answer ....

Your answer ....

The correct answer ....

♡♡♡♡♡♡♡♡♡♡♡♡♡♡♡♡♡♡♡♡♡♡♡♡

10. (Your own question) ....

....

Your friend's answer ....

The correct answer ....

Your answer ....

The correct answer ....

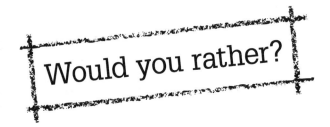

IF YOU HAD THE CHANCE TO SPEND SOME TIME WITH ALFIE, WHAT WOULD YOU DO? TAKE A LOOK AT THE ACTIVITIES LISTED BELOW AND TICK THE BOX NEXT TO YOUR PREFERRED CHOICE. TAKE YOUR TIME. YOU HAVE SOME VERY TRICKY DECISIONS TO MAKE!

Would you rather ...

Take Nala for a walk with Alfie? ⬌ Have Alfie help you choose your own puppy?

Have Alfie give you a shout-out in a video? ⬌ Help Alfie edit one of his daily blogs?

Go shopping with Alfie and Zoe? ⬌ Go on a spa day with Zoe?

Have Alfie sign one of his books for you? ⬌ Have Alfie retweet a message from you?

Set Alfie and Marcus your own World Record Challenge? ⬌ Take part in a World Record Challenge with Alfie?

Go to a book-launch party as Alfie's VIP guest? Have Alfie as your guest at your birthday party?

Design a T-shirt for Alfie to wear in a video? Have Alfie design a special one-off T-shirt for you?

Make a video where Alfie restyles your hair? Make a video where you do Alfie's makeup for him?

Take part in a Truth or Dare video with Alfie? Have Alfie answer all your questions in a video?

Have a day out in Brighton with Alfie and his pals? Take Alfie ten-pin bowling with your friends?

Choose the title of Alfie's next book? Have Alfie name his new puppy after you?

Challenge Alfie to a banana-eating contest? Have a whipped-cream pie-fight with Alfie?

Choose what Alfie wears in his latest video? Get Alfie to choose a new outfit for you?

What's the word?

CAN YOU FIND ALL THE ALFIE-RELATED WORDS OR
PHRASES IN THE WORD SEARCH OPPOSITE? THEY COULD
BE READ FORWARD, BACKWARD, UP, DOWN, ACROSS,
OR DIAGONALLY. TRACK DOWN ANY YOU JUST
CAN'T FIND ON **PAGE 94**.

POINTLESSBLOG

ZOELLA

ZALFIE

TANYA

MARCUS

BRIGHTON

NALA

CASPAR LEE

YOUTUBE

JOE SUGG

F	K	N	P	B	W	K	T	G	K	E	S	U	W	E
T	L	F	X	H	S	T	R	C	V	D	T	I	A	B
H	F	A	G	D	M	A	O	U	N	N	S	G	N	R
U	B	W	Y	A	V	N	M	Q	P	A	O	P	E	H
Q	T	I	E	N	J	Y	Z	O	E	L	L	A	D	S
D	E	O	Q	U	V	A	B	I	B	A	K	E	J	U
Z	D	C	S	R	L	R	Z	S	C	T	I	E	U	M
H	S	Z	L	F	N	F	S	U	B	G	L	S	V	B
I	E	P	I	M	T	E	D	C	O	W	D	R	J	Y
Y	B	E	A	W	L	L	B	R	I	G	H	T	O	N
G	U	R	J	T	F	C	R	A	W	N	R	K	E	K
B	T	F	N	W	Y	D	O	M	V	T	H	A	S	B
R	U	I	H	K	N	A	U	P	N	G	E	F	U	A
J	O	V	Z	E	E	L	R	A	P	S	A	C	G	M
P	Y	M	A	K	D	E	T	C	N	P	S	X	G	N

Stars in your eyes

OBVIOUSLY YOU THINK ALFIE IS NUMBER ONE, BUT HERE'S YOUR CHANCE TO RATE EVERYTHING ABOUT HIM AND WORK OUT EXACTLY WHAT MAKES HIM SO PERFECT. COLOR IN THE STARS TO GIVE A STAR RATING FROM ONE TO FIVE, DEPENDING ON HOW IMPORTANT EACH OF ALFIE'S VERY SPECIAL QUALITIES IS TO YOU.

Star rating

No biggie

Quite like

Just love this about him

Soooooo Alfie

Essential Alfie

1. Alfie's hairstyle is lush.

2. Alfie always wears the best jumpers, shirts, and T-shirts.

3. Alfie has the best smile.

4. Alfie's laugh is adorable.

5. Alfie is definitely the funniest YouTuber.

6. Alfie has created the most entertaining challenges.

7. Alfie does the best impressions of his vlogger pals.

8. Alfie's gaming videos are the best online.

9. Alfie's videos are very informative.

10. Alfie is a really good cook.

11. Alfie is always on time.

12. Alfie keeps his flat clean and tidy.

13. Alfie buys the best presents for other people.

14. Alfie is a great boyfriend and is always very romantic with Zoe.

15. Alfie is always very kind and caring.

16. Alfie's solo videos are better than his collaborations.

17. Alfie has the cutest little lisp.

18. Alfie and Zoe's place is amazing.

ALFIE ISN'T ALWAYS THE COOLEST GUY IN THE WORLD. HE'S HAD PLENTY OF EMBARRASSING MISHAPS AND TOTAL-CRINGE MOMENTS, BUT HE'S ALWAYS WILLING TO TELL HIS VIEWERS ABOUT THEM AND LAUGH AT HIS OWN MISTAKES. CAN YOU TELL WHICH OF THE STORIES BELOW ARE GENUINE AND WHICH ONES HAVE BEEN INVENTED? ANSWERS ARE ON **PAGE 94**.

1. When Alfie was 13, he cut off all his hair and completely shaved his head for charity. When he saw the end result, he started to cry.

☐ True ☐ False

2. On the first day at his secondary school, Alfie wore a formal suit and sunglasses because he wanted everyone to think he was cool.

☐ True ☐ False

3. Alfie's friends once persuaded him to have his bum cheeks waxed.

☐ True ☐ False

4. When Alfie was five years old, he entered a talent competition at his primary school singing a song from Disney's *Beauty and the Beast*. The most embarrassing thing was that he was dressed as Belle.

☐ True   ☐ False

5. When Alfie attended his first school dance, he turned up dressed like a pirate because his friends had told him it was a costume party. It wasn't. Alfie went straight home and missed the dance.

☐ True   ☐ False

6. Alfie once said that his favorite chat-up line is "Can I borrow your phone because I said I'd call my mum when I'd fallen in love." But he quickly confirmed that he'd never use such a cheesy line in real life. Phew!

☐ True   ☐ False

7. While he was making the "Eggs To The Face" video with Marcus Butler, Alfie's mom caught them in the middle of filming and gave Alfie a telling-off for wasting her eggs.

☐ True   ☐ False

8. Alfie says his biggest cringe moment happened when he was about six years old while swimming with his parents. Alfie got out of the water and walked around the entire edge of the pool before he realized his white trunks had become completely see-through.

☐ True   ☐ False

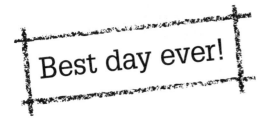

GETTING STARTED AS A BLOGGER IS EASY. ALL YOU HAVE TO DO IS WRITE ABOUT THE THINGS YOU FIND INTERESTING OR ENJOY DOING AND HOPEFULLY OTHERS WILL WANT TO JOIN IN THE FUN TOO. WHY DON'T YOU TRY WRITING A "MY BEST DAY EVER" BLOG? THINK ABOUT SOME OF THE BEST THINGS THAT HAVE HAPPENED TO ALFIE AND USE THEM TO INSPIRE A STORY ABOUT YOUR OWN EXPERIENCES.

List some of the amazing places you've visited:

....

....

....

List a few of the fun games or activities you did when you were there:

....

....

....

Who were you with when you had your "best day ever"? Why were you glad they were there?

....

....

....

Now write a blog called "My Best Day Ever." Show how a happy memory can make any day better.

....

....

....

....

....

....

....

....

....

....

....

Perfect partners

DO YOU THINK YOU'VE GOT WHAT IT TAKES TO BE ONE OF ALFIE'S BEST PALS? TRY THE QUIZ BELOW TO FIND OUT IF YOU COULD BE A PART OF ALFIE'S GANG.... THERE MIGHT EVEN BE A SPARE SEAT FOR YOU ON "THE CREW." WORK OUT YOUR SCORE ON **PAGE 94**.

1. You're supposed to be meeting Alfie at his flat at midday. Your journey took less time than you expected and you turn up a couple of hours early. What should you do?

   a. Kill time by having a coffee and return to the flat at midday with Nando's takeaway for lunch.

   b. Film yourself waiting outside Alfie's flat. It will make a good daily vlog segment.

   c. Keep ringing the doorbell until Alfie answers. You know he loves getting up early, so he won't mind.

2. Alfie is hoping you can organize a fun day out for you both. What do you suggest?

   a. A full day shopping for clothes

   b. Going to see One Direction in concert

   c. You've bought Alfie some cool new gaming gadgets. Unfortunately, there are no instructions in the box and you'll need to spend the next few hours trying to work out how it all works.

3. You've arranged for you both to visit London Zoo on your day out. What fun activities have you planned?

a. You and Alfie are going to spend time feeding and playing with the monkeys inside their enclosure.

b. You've arranged for Alfie to spend the afternoon in the invertebrates house, where he can handle some of the biggest spiders in the world.

c. You and Alfie will be introduced to several different species of snake.

4. You go for lunch at Alfie's favorite restaurant. Which of these things would make Alfie happiest?

a. You are sitting next to a man who eats very loudly.

b. Taylor Swift is sitting at the next table.

c. The restaurant has just introduced sticky toffee pudding to the menu.

5. After your meal, you decide to go see a movie. What do you choose?

a. A Harry Potter movie marathon

b. A sing-along version of *The Lion King*

c. *The Truman Show*

6. When you take your seats at the cinema, what's the worst thing that could happen next?

a. The couple next to Alfie starts kissing really loudly.

b. The only chocs on sale at the concessions stand are Terry's Chocolate Oranges.

c. Alfie's seat number is 13.

7. Zoe turns up and she seems a little upset. What do you do?

   a. Ask Zoe if she minds letting you film her crying for your daily vlog.

   b. Give Alfie and Zoe some space and leave them to spend time on their own.

   c. Buy Alfie and Zoe ice cream.

8. What are Alfie's favorite characteristics in other people?

   a. Smiling a lot

   b. Knowing how to get away with telling lies

   c. Being really funny

Are you perfect partners?

If you scored 10 or under: Do you even know who Alfie is? You know what you need to do. Get online and find out what you've been missing.

If you scored 11 to 18: Not bad—you seem to know your stuff, but you made a few mistakes. Keep watching Alfie's videos and you never know, there might be a best-bud vacancy in the future.

If you scored more than 18: Alfie has made space for you at his top table. You two will get on like a house on fire. Marcus and Caspar better watch out, there's a new BFF on the scene.

Laugh out loud!

ALFIE ALWAYS HAS A LOT TO SAY BUT HE SOMETIMES GETS A LITTLE CONFUSED. HERE ARE A FEW OF ALFIE'S CRAZIEST QUOTES.

"I don't like spiders.... It's when you see a spider on the floor or on the wall or in your bed, you turn back around for half a second, you look back, and it's gone. You're left sitting there thinking, 'This spider's going to frickin' kill me while I'm asleep.'"

"That looks disgusting. It's literally done a poo.... I thought making burgers was meant to be nice."

"I don't like crabs, guys. They don't like me and I don't like them. It's cool. It's like a mutual agreement not to like each other in life and I think that's fine."

"We're all chillin' outside ... it's raining loads now, so we're all in some like outside little hut thingy with wheels. What's it called? A caravan."

BEFORE HE BECAME ONE OF THE MOST FAMOUS FACES ON THE INTERNET, ALFIE WAS JUST A NORMAL KID LIKE EVERYBODY ELSE AND HE HAD THE SAME WORRIES AND PROBLEMS MOST PEOPLE HAVE AT SCHOOL. HERE ARE A FEW OF ALFIE'S SCHOOL-DAYS FACTS AND MEMORIES.

1. Alfie says he never joined any particular clique when he was at school. He thinks it is much better to be friends with as many different types of people as possible.

2. Alfie appeared in three different musicals during his school days: *West Side Story*, *Fiddler on the Roof*, and *Jesus Christ Superstar*.

3. Alfie says he never pretended to be ill to get out of going to school.

4. The subjects Alfie studied at college were math, geography, chemistry, and biology.

5. Alfie was a keen gymnast for about six years. He reached a high enough level to compete in several school and regional tournaments.

6. When it came time to study for exams, Alfie remembers that even if he had 30 days to do the work, he would always leave it to the last minute and try to cram everything into two days. Alfie now thinks he could have pushed himself and achieved more in his exams.

7. Alfie says he had his first girlfriend when he was about 15. It lasted for about a year. He admits that he didn't actually have another relationship until he started dating Zoe when he was 19. He says it's best not to feel pressure to date just because your friends are doing it.

8. When Alfie was at school, all his friends started experimenting with smoking cigarettes. He says he realized it was an unhealthy thing to do and decided he didn't even want to try it. Alfie admits he experienced a lot of peer pressure during this time and advises people to make up their own minds about the things they do or don't do.

9. Alfie hated wearing his school uniform. He was a bit of a rebel and used to break the uniform rules by wearing black skinny jeans to school instead of baggy, straight-legged trousers.

10. Alfie's most important piece of advice about school days is to try and keep everything in perspective.

Blog planner

WHEN ALFIE STARTED VLOGGING, HE DIDN'T REALLY KNOW WHAT HE WANTED TO TALK ABOUT—HE DID CALL IT THE POINTLESSBLOG AFTER ALL! IF YOU WANT TO CREATE YOUR OWN BLOG OR VLOG, IT MIGHT BE A BETTER IDEA TO THINK IT THROUGH CAREFULLY BEFORE YOU GET STARTED. HERE ARE SOME USEFUL QUESTIONS TO ASK YOURSELF AND SOME TIPS TO HELP YOU PLAN YOUR FIRST BLOG/VLOG.

1. "What do I want to write or talk about?"

Write down a list of your favorite subjects at school, hobbies you enjoy, or things you know a lot about. You want other people to be as excited about the subject as you are, so make sure it's interesting or fun.

....

....

....

....

....

....

....

2.   "What do I think other people like to read about or
watch videos about? What do *I* like to read and watch?"

....

....

....

....

....

....

3.   Are there any subjects that appear on both lists?
Maybe your blog/vlog should be about one of those.

....

....

....

4.   "Can I think of a cool name for my blog/vlog?"

Make a list of words that are related to your topic and
see if they give you any ideas. Can any of them be
turned into a phrase or longer word?

....

....

....

....

....

5. "Do I want to vlog on my own or with someone else?"

You might want your own personality to shine through or you might enjoy making blogs or vlogs with your best friend or a group of mates. Or the answer might be to compromise, like Alfie, by having special guests in your vlogs from time to time.

6. "How often do I want to vlog?"

Alfie has always been keen to keep in touch with his fans on a regular basis. And now that he has millions of followers around the world, he tries to post daily blogs, as well as weekly updates and gaming videos. Be realistic about how much free time you have. Never put vlogging before your schoolwork or college assignments, as you never know what might happen in the future. Write regular times when you can work on blogs or vlogs here:

....

....

When you are starting out, it's always advisable to post regularly—maybe once or twice a week—at the same time each week. Your followers will know when to expect a new post. If you miss your deadlines, you're likely to start losing your viewers.

7. "How long should my videos/blogs be?"

When you are starting out, your videos and posts need to be short and to the point. Give your viewers a good idea of what your posts will be about and some hints about what might be coming up in the future. Keep things simple and clear. Editing is your friend. No one wants to watch long pauses or sections where nothing is happening.

8. "How do I keep things interesting?"

The success of your blog will rely completely on you keeping things interesting and fun for your viewers. You need to come across as confident and relaxed, so talk about what you know and practice before you start. If you are excited about your posts, it will show and your viewers are more likely to be excited too. You're only as good as your last post. If you start to lose interest, so will your viewers.

9. "How do I let people know about my blog or videos?"

Start by sending invites to your friends and family. Ask them to share with people they know who might be interested in your posts. Soon you will start to see your numbers grow. The more you post, and the better the feedback, the bigger your blog is likely to get. Set up social-media accounts for your blog using your blogger name. A Facebook page or Twitter account is a great place for you to interact with your followers and let them know more about you and your blogs or videos. You will be able to let them know when you've added new content and get instant feedback. Get in touch with other vloggers. They might have advice or give you tips.

Don't send your posts or videos to people you don't know, or ask for shares and likes from people who haven't asked to join your community. You don't want to appear desperate or too pushy.

10. "What are my chances of success?"

With vlogging, you are in control of what you do and there are no limits. If you come up with a good idea and deliver it in an interesting and unique way, there's no reason why you can't be as successful as Alfie and Zoe or any of the other vloggers out there. If you put some time and effort into it, you could have a lot of fun and make it a big success. Remember: Everyone started by posting his or her first video or blog. Where it goes from there is up to you. Write your ideas for your first blog or vlog here:

....

....

....

....

....

....

....

....

Give it a try ...

IF YOU WANT TO BECOME A POPULAR BLOGGER
LIKE ALFIE OR ZOE, YOU NEED TO DEVELOP YOUR
OWN STYLE OF WRITING AND CREATE SOMETHING
SPECIAL AND UNIQUE. YOU SHOULD PRACTICE BY
WRITING ABOUT THE THINGS YOU DO EVERY DAY
FOR A WHOLE WEEK. THINK ABOUT WHAT MIGHT
BE MOST INTERESTING FOR OTHER PEOPLE OR
THE FUNNIEST THINGS THAT HAPPENED TO YOU.
THERE ARE A FEW TIPS AND HELPFUL HINTS BELOW.
REMEMBER: PRACTICE MAKES PERFECT!

1. Make a list of the three most memorable things you did on each day of the past week.

Monday

1. ....

2. ....

3. ....

Tuesday

1. ....

2. ....

3. ....

Wednesday

1. ....

2. ....

3. ....

Thursday

1. ....

2. ....

3. ....

Friday

1. ....

2. ....

3. ....

Saturday

1. ....

2. ....

3. ....

Sunday

1. ....

2. ....

3. ....

2. List the friends and family you spent time with this week and who you might want to include in your blog.

....

....

....

3. Write down a few of the funniest things your friends said to you this week.

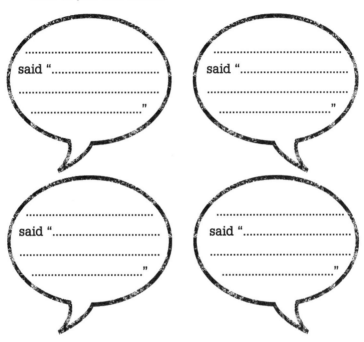

said "..
....
...."

said "..
....
...."

said "..
....
...."

said "..
....
...."

Turn the funny or interesting things people have said into short paragraphs or stories. Imagine other people reading your story and make sure it all makes sense if they don't know any of you or where you are.

4. Now it's time to start writing a blog about your week. You can write about the whole week or each individual day. Include some funny or interesting stories or events and how you felt about them. And remember: Other people are going to read this, so it's best to stick to the truth. Keep writing and have fun!

OMG! World records!

ALFIE AND MARCUS (TEAM MALFIE) HAVE BEEN
CHALLENGED TO TAKE PART IN DOZENS OF GUINNESS
WORLD RECORDS OVER ON THEIR RECORD SLAM
CHANNEL—THEY'VE EVEN MANAGED TO BREAK A FEW.
CAN YOU TELL WHICH OF THE WORLD RECORDS LISTED
BELOW ARE REAL AND WHICH ARE FAKE? THERE ARE
EXTRA POINTS IF YOU CAN SPOT WHICH ONES ALFIE AND
MARCUS ACTUALLY SUCCEEDED IN BEATING. TURN TO
PAGE 95 FOR YOUR SCORE.

1. Popping 50 balloons in less than eight seconds.

☐ True   ☐ False   ☐ Success

2. Building a pyramid using 20 empty tin cans in the
shortest possible time.

☐ True   ☐ False   ☐ Success

3. Fastest time to completely wrap up another person
like a Christmas present.

☐ True   ☐ False   ☐ Success

4. In the "Bra Removing Challenge" the boys had to see how many times they could put on and remove a bra in one minute.

☐ True   ☐ False   ☐ Success

5. Alfie and Marcus had to remove the shells of and eat as many hard-boiled eggs as they could in three minutes.

☐ True   ☐ False   ☐ Success

6. Peel and eat more than eight bananas in one minute.

☐ True   ☐ False   ☐ Success

7. Most times you can bounce a tennis ball on alternate sides of a tennis racket for one minute.

☐ True   ☐ False   ☐ Success

8. Fastest time to remove a pair of socks and put them back on the opposite feet.

☐ True   ☐ False   ☐ Success

9. Popping the most party poppers in 30 seconds.

☐ True   ☐ False   ☐ Success

10. Make and eat as many hot dogs in a bun as they could in three minutes.

☐ True   ☐ False   ☐ Success

SUPPOSE YOU RECEIVED THE MYSTERIOUS INVITATION BELOW. WHERE WOULD YOU GO AND WHEN? FILL IN THE GAPS AND TURN TO **PAGE 95** TO SEE IF YOU'VE CRACKED IT.

Place: the town where Alfie was born and still lives.

At: a famous landmark built over 200 years ago that Alfie talked about in his "My Future Home" video.

Date: the month of Alfie's birth and the date that is the same as Alfie's age when he started vlogging.

Time: in the afternoon, the same as the number of brothers and sisters Alfie has.

....

is invited to

The ...., ...
on .... of .... at .... pm

to celebrate the brilliant career of Alfie Deyes!

All the answers

R U his no. 1 fan?
Pages 6–9

1.	b	**4.**	c	**7.**	b	**10.**	b
2.	a	**5.**	b	**8.**	a	**11.**	c
3.	c	**6.**	c	**9.**	a	**12.**	a

Favorite things
Pages 10–11

1.	b	**6.**	a
2.	c	**7.**	c
3.	b	**8.**	b
4.	b	**9.**	a
5.	c		

Meet the vloggers
Pages 16–18

1.	Zoe Sugg	**6.**	Tanya Burr
2.	Caspar Lee	**7.**	Jim Chapman
3.	Jim Chapman	**8.**	Caspar Lee
4.	Zoe Sugg	**9.**	Tanya Burr
5.	Marcus Butler		

True or false?
Page 19

1. True
2. False—it happened to a friend of Alfie's.
3. True
4. True

Love it or hate it?
Pages 20–21

1. True
2. True
3. False
4. True
5. False
6. True
7. True
8. True
9. False
10. True
11. False

Quirky questions
Pages 30–31

1. E
2. B
3. G
4. D
5. C
6. I

Young at heart
Pages 39–41

1. c
2. a
3. b
4. b
5. b
6. a
7. b
8. b
9. a
10. b
11. a
12. b

What vlog?
Pages 42–43

1. Nala, his dog, in "Home Alone With My Puppy!!"
2. His moustache in "Having A Baby!!"
3. Sugary American candy in "My Car Is FROZEN..."
4. Pizza in "Finding A Burglar In The Flat..."
5. Smoking cigarettes in "Making Friends & Peer Pressure"
6. Marcus Butler in "We Need To Have A Talk..."

Up close and personal
Pages 46–48

All about Alfie

1. Brighton
2. Nala
3. *The Pointless Book*
4. Virgo
5. 2009
6. Twenty-nine
7. Verified on Twitter
8. September

All about Zalfie

1. Percy and Pippin
2. *Girl Online*
3. "Zalfie."
4. August
5. Younger
6. thoughts. fashion. beauty.
7. Anne Frank's *The Diary of a Young Girl*
8. In a dream

All about Alfie's family and friends

1. Poppy
2. Jim Chapman, Marcus Butler, or Caspar Lee
3. Vlogmas
4. Kingston University
5. Marcus Butler
6. Sprinkleofglitter
7. Superdrug
8. Amity Fest

Did you know that?
Pages 53–55

1. True
2. True
3. False
4. False
5. True
6. True
7. False
8. True
9. True
10. False
11. True
12. True
13. True
14. False
15. True
16. True
17. False
18. True
19. False
20. True
21. False
22. False
23. True

What's the word?
Pages 64–65

F	K	N	P	B	W	K	T	G	K	E	S	U	W	E
T	L	F	X	H	S	T	R	C	V	D	T	I	A	B
H	F	A	G	D	M	A	O	U	N	N	S	G	N	R
U	B	W	Y	A	V	N	M	Q	P	A	O	P	E	H
Q	T	I	E	N	J	Y	Z	O	E	L	A	D	S
D	E	O	Q	U	V	A	B	I	B	A	K	E	J	U
Z	D	C	S	R	L	R	Z	B	C	T	I	E	U	M
H	S	Z	L	F	N	F	S	U	B	G	L	S	V	B
I	E	P	M	T	C	D	C	O	W	D	R	Y
Y	B	E	A	W	L	L	B	A	I	C	H	T	O	N
G	U	R	J	T	F	C	R	A	W	N	R	K	E	K
B	T	F	N	W	Y	D	O	M	V	T	H	A	S	B
R	U	I	H	K	N	A	U	P	N	G	E	F	U	A
J	D	V	Z	E	E	L	R	A	P	S	A	C	C	M
R	Y	M	A	K	D	E	T	C	N	P	S	X	C	N

Cringe!
Pages 70–71

1. True
2. False
3. True

4. False
5. False
6. True

7. False
8. True

Perfect partners
Pages 74–75

1. a.3 b.2 c.1
2. a.2 b.3 c.1
3. a.3 b.1 c.2

4. a.1 b.3 c.2
5. a.2 b.1 c.3
6. a.1 b.3 c.2

7. a.1 b.3 c.2
8. a.2 b.3 c.1

OMG! World records!
Pages 88–89

1.	True, no	**5.**	False
2.	True, yes	**6.**	True, no
3.	True, no	**7.**	True, yes
4.	True, yes (matched but didn't beat the record)	**8.**	False
		9.	True, yes
		10.	True, no

See ya!
Page 90

```
..............................................................

                        is invited to
              The Royal Pavillion, Brighton
                on 15th of August at 2 pm

    to celebrate the brilliant career of Alfie Deyes!
```

ISBN: 978-1-4494-7185-9